# Way to Go – Spiritual Living

# Way to Go

## *Spiritual Living*

*JUSTINA NWAKAMMA*

# Way to Go – Spiritual Living

Published by Fountain of Life Publisher's House

P. O. Box 922612 Norcross, GA 30010
Phone: 404-936-3989
Please Email Manuscripts to: publish@pariceparker.biz
For all book orders including wholesale email: sales@pariceparker.biz
To request author email: author@pariceparker.biz
www.pariceparker.biz

Fountain of Life Publishing House is committed to excellence in the publishing industry. The Company reflects the philosophy established by the founder, based on Psalm 68:11, *"The Lord gave the word and great was the company of those who published it."*

*Book design copyright © 2016 by Parice C Parker. All rights reserved.*
*Authored by JUSTINA NWAKAMMA*
*Cover Design by Parice C. Parker*
*Interior design by Parice C. Parker*
*Editor: FOLPH Editor's Team*

*Published in the United States of America*

ISBN: 978-0692745670

# Way to Go

## Table of Contents

*JUSTINA NWAKAMMA*

# Introduction

The author of this book was born and raised in Nigeria to a Christian family where my father worked as a pastor of the Apostolic Church with my mother supporting him and the family and preaching the gospel from one town to another. Then we grew up to become adults and by God's grace moved to America to join my wonderful husband Chris and we are blessed with four children. My Dad was an ordained pastor of The Apostolic church he was a preacher and loved the Lord and God used him to perform miracles and many churches got converted from his preaching of salvation. A lot of souls were won for the Lord because of his work. He prayed for sick people and they were healed and many more miracles took place from his faith in God. I grew up with my siblings even though we did not have lots of money but we had the peace of God within us and the grace of God was sufficient and my parents raised us their six children with the fear of God growing up.

As a Teenager growing up I was born in the home of a Christian and I learnt respect and obedience from day one. I was coming back from an errand one day in my village in Umuahia Abia State of Nigeria I passed by a Church and the building did not look right to me. I wanted the building to be really big and magnificent but it was not due to lack of money. So I prayed and said to myself I wish God can help me go overseas or travel to American so I can get a job and make some money to help this church. Little did I know, God heard that prayer. As in the book of Mark chapter 2, verse 8 where the Bible says that the Lord knows our thoughts. So, it happened.

After my nursing and midwifery training which took four years to complete, I met my present husband who I am still married to today. The Lord has been blessing me so much physically, emotionally, financially and spiritually. I thought about what I could do for God who has been good to me, and who brought me this far. He is the one who has kept my family together even when my father died not of old age and to make matters worse,I was a teenager and no job, not able to help my family. But we continue to worship and I thought what I can do to show my appreciation to God for sustaining me as the first daughter with all the family stress and God was able to sustain our family. Then it occurred to me to write a book so that people can also appreciate God in their life and I want people to know and understand that spiritual living is the *Way to Go.*

*JUSTINA NWAKAMMA*

# *Chapter One*

# *The Grace of God*

The grace of God has carried us through all these years. Then when the thoughts of writing a book came to me I did not know how or what to write. I began to search and pray then I had some revelations about book titles, and this is how I came to write this book. The most important thing that I want people to know is that in the world we live in today, there is so much confusion and chaos. There is so much anxiety, people have many questions and wants answers and solutions to problems going on around us, and sometimes things happen for no reason. We cannot comprehend why things happen the way they do, and some answers are still far fetched. Everyone has a much fear and anxiety of some sort not knowing what the future holds in our economy, job situations, marital problems, and criminal activities on the increase just to mention a few and fluctuations in every other area of our lives. We experience chaos and suffering all around us and there is no hope. And everyone is wondering what shall we do to make things better in our nations, school system, job and economic situations? Living in a world that is unpredictable with social and economic hardship.

It is also worth knowing that we have a solution to our problem. This is achieved by letting the *Prince of Peace* who is the Lord, Jesus Christ be the Lord and reign in our lives and bring about the everlasting solution. He is also the one who promised us a heavenly home of many mansions which he prepared for all who love Him. This permanent home where our Father is the builder is special in the sense that the only people that will inhabit this home is the ones cleansed by the blood of the Lamb, and those with pure hearts. Those who are made spotless by his blood will inhabit such a home. In order to habit this heavenly home, there are preparations we are required to make. Just as it is required, for one to pass an examination, you have to study. In order to have a job or work, you have to go to school and acquire knowledge to get education in the field that you'd want to pursue. There are requirements needed to obtain a degree. There is also a prerequisite to be completed to be accepted into a college. I have a son preparing to enter college, and he is trying to apply to different schools. Every school has different requirements. In order to get where you want to be, one has to be compliant and do what is required at that point in time to achieve your goals. As one gets ready to move from an apartment to a house, there are preparations and requirements that go with it. At least one requirement is to have good credit or be able to have some type of down payment available. People who move from an apartment into a house knows how important it is to save some money for down payment.


Some careers, special courses have to be taken to obtain the degree to fit the job. Most job have requirements to be fulfilled before one can be accepted. For instance, if you refuse to take a drug test, some corporations will not offer you the job. So it is with our Father in heaven, who loves us so much to give his only begotten son to come and die on the cross in order to save us from our sins. The Bible says, he who know no sins came to die for sinners. Is this not wonderful love from our father? In order to be qualified for the heavenly home, one of the requirements is to accept the Lord, Jesus as the Lord and personal savior. The Bible says confession is made by mouth. Confessing your sins with your mouth and believing in your heart that Jesus is Lord then accepting Him as Lord and the personal savior, you will be saved. Confession is made by the mouth and acceptance by the heart for salvation to be obtained. You see, the Lord does not force any of us to accept Him. He is always pleading with us. The Bible says behold he stands at the door knocking and if anyone opens his or her heart , he will come in. As the *Creator* and *Maker*, He has the power to force our heart doors to open. He does not want us to perish. Acceptance by our willingness through our own self decision. He is encouraging us to open the door of our hearts so he can come in and dwell in our hearts just like going to someone house when the door is locked. No one can enter into another man's house if the door is locked. It is only home breakers who will force the door open or it may be the home owner lost the key to the house, then it will be forced open. This is not so with our heavenly father. We have to open the door of our hearts to him to let him in.

Another thing to consider is this. What type of heart does he live in? The fact is, he cannot live in an impure heart. This is a heart that thinks evil or devises evil things from the heart.

## Way to Go – Spiritual Living

We are called children of God because our father is holy. We are required to be holy in every area of our lives including the way we talk, act and live our lives. God is the owner of our lives and he is the creator of heaven and earth therefore we should fear and respect him at all times and teach our children and grandchildren to do the same. This is why when we accept the Lord as our personal savior then the Holy Spirit takes over our life directing our paths.

In this book, the author wants everyone to understand the importance of accepting the Lord Jesus in our lives. It does not matter the academic qualification, socio-economic status, color of our skin, age or the language you speak. We all are God's children bought by the precious blood of Jesus Christ. The result of accepting Jesus is to have eternal life, and miss hell.

We don't want to be with Satan because he hates us. Satan came to kill and destroy us. He is a deceiver and has been even from the time of Adam and Eve till this present time. Satan will tell all type of lies because he is the father of lies. He will deceive any one that he finds vulnerable. That is why the Bible encourages us to resist the devil, and he will flee from you. No one wants to live with his or her enemy. We must be aware of his devices, and flee from his temptations. He deceives people by telling them some things contrary to the will of God. Satan wants people to go to hell with him but if you accept the Lord in your life salvation is yours and you will not be close to him. Jesus came to give life to us and give it more abundantly the Bible says. There is no condemnation for those that believe in the name of Jesus Christ. As Jesus promised us in the Bible, He is going to prepare a place for us and he will come back and gather us for himself. The bible says that God is not a liar or son of man that he should repent or change his mind. The words of the Lord are so powerful that it cannot return to him void. His word is like a two-edged sword that can pierce through the heart and discern thoughts.

The devil has many tactics to deceive people that is why he brings all kind of worldly pleasures to attract and trick us. Satan wants us to postpone salvation until we get ready. Sometimes, the devil brings discouragement to our hearts and wants us to be disobedient to the promises of the Lord. Sometimes, I hear people say, "Oh, I want to enjoy my youth. I will serve God when I grow old." This book is to advise everyone that salvation is freely offered to both old and young. We need the Lord in our younger years so he can lead us through the older years. Youth are being encouraged to accept him today because he says, "Behold today is the acceptable day and today is the day of salvation." The thing is, Satan wants us to wait and keep postponing salvation. Please do not keep giving excuses why you cannot accept the Lord in your life today.

Satan came to kill and destroy that is why he continues to bring confusion. He will not allow people to make a decision to follow Christ because he knows when Christ is in you satan will run away. Jesus is the light. The darkness will always disappear when light comes in because both cannot work together, the darkness always gets out when light comes in. Have you ever tried to come into your house when it's dark? You will notice as soon as the light is turned on the darkness disappears. This is what happens when one accepts Christ the darkness cannot stand the light. Jesus said, "I am the way, the truth and the life". When we accept him we have life but if we don't we do not have life. No one comes to the father except by me Jesus said. No one knows the way to heaven. It's only Jesus who knows the way. He is the way, the truth and the life. Please don't keep giving excuses, accept the Lord as you read this book. Remember, the Bible says, today is the day of salvation and the day of acceptance. It is very important to make a decision today. It will not profit us anything to gain the world and loose our soul Just as we make time to make money or attend party's, we need to make time for our spiritual life. God does not want any of us to perish he is calling for everyone to repent, and come unto him. The devil has deceived many people through what the eyes can see or what ears can hear using the things of this world to deceive us. To be  citizen of heaven, we are to be born again and accept the salvation offered to us freely. For one to become a citizen of a country there are some requirement to be fulfilled so it is with being a child of God, and having the aspiration of heavenly citizenship.

## Way to Go – Spiritual Living

God made us in his likeness, and image. If he did not make us, we will not be here and if he had chosen to make us like a tree or stone we would be same no one can change it. The problem is that man has disobeyed God by our actions and behaviors. The whole thing is geared by the devil who constantly deceives us, and leads people to sin all the time.

This is why it is important to allow the Holy Spirit to dwell, empower and use us to produce all the fruits of the spirit. It will be able to break all the yolk of sin. Sin has a lot of weight and tends to bring us down, but righteousness exalts a nation. Take for instance the issue of cheating on men and women. A man/ woman that cheats on their spouse is not walking with God rather he or she is walking with Satan because such person is fulfilling the desire of the devil. When the bible says " Husbands love your wives," as Christ loved the church, and gave his life for us. Same goes to women. On the other hand, wives should respect their husbands, and let them be the head that God wants them to be. Give peace a chance in your relationship. Divorce is so rampant in the world today due to various reasons but the only solution is to let the *Prince of Peace* come into your life before, during and within the parameters of marriage.

Honoring God in all we do even teaching our kids the way of the Lord when they grow up they will not forsake it. Children also have a part to play to honor the Lord. "Obey your father and mother so your days may be long." Every word of God is so powerful, and means a lot to us. The word of God has everything we need to live and survive only if we can listen and obey. It teaches love, kindness and even how to respond to one another. A man that does not provide for his family, and put food on the table is not performing what the Lord wants him to do. Men must love your wives as Christ loved the church, and also provide for them "Husbands love your wives." Provide for your family. Men should not be lazy. They need to go out there and gather for their family. They should not abandon the wives to raise children single handedly because it is not meant for one person to raise kids, there has to be two people. The bible says "Two are better than one." You can Goggle all the advantages of working with two rather than one person. The same goes for both men and women. It is high time we allow God to rule in our marriages. If you have a wife, the Lord is expecting the ladies to be loyal, humble and submit to their husbands whom God placed to be the head of the family and work together as a team. Ladies, please help our men. Sometimes we have to teach them stuff because some of them don't know. I am not bragging, but they lack knowledge and understanding will destroy a person. This is why God let you marry whoever you are married to.

Also, raising kids is a big responsibility that God gave to us. We need to seek God to give us wisdom, understanding and financial capabilities to take care of these children who are entrusted in our care. Also, a woman doing the same is not right. We need to show respect to God in our relationships with one another. God is expecting for us to allow Him to be the Lord of our marriage and family relations. We all need His grace to survive. Disobedience is from Satan, but the Holy Spirit came to help us obey God. By listening to the small voice in your heart for the do's and don'ts, it will help. It is only those washed by the blood of the Lamb that will inherit the Kingdom of God. Salvation is a free gift. We may not know how much it cost Him to send Christ on the cross. The Holy Spirit helps us to accept him. In John 1:12, the bible says it is "he that gives power to become children of God". His Holy Spirit in us helps, encourages, and comforts us in all situations. When we accept the Lord in our lives, then we are given the power to become sons and daughters of God. There is power in the blood of Jesus to break every yolk of sin, poverty, sickness, disease infirmity, including alcoholism and drug addiction. We need the power of the Holy Spirit to break all these yolks of sin. We cannot continue to sin, and expect grace to abound.

Some people drink alcohol and smoke cigarettes. Some do some fun loving activities such as partying, and drinking. Some even get intoxicated from consuming large amounts of beer or other substances especially when the body has had enough, we have to allow the Holy Spirit to guide our lives. There are certain foods  you may not like to eat and the things that you loved to do before,  you may not do again because your spiritual eyes will be opened. It is our spiritual journey. Our Heavenly Father wants us to be filled with the Holy Spirit. Why? One may ask. The answer is simple. We are what we eat or consume. If people eat healthy foods such as vegetables in our diet, I believe they will be healthy and get all the benefits of being healthy. On the other hand, if we eat junk food the body cannot get enough nourishment doing that. Likewise, living a life filled with the Holy Spirit or in other words allowing the Holy Spirit to direct our lives attract the grace and mercy of God. Allowing the Holy Spirit to guide our lives and being sensitive to Him by acceptance of Christ is good.

God's expectation is for us to live for him and more so, we were created to worship Him and can do so by being obedient and reverencing to His words. To be spirit filled is to have wisdom, and understanding. The Holy Spirit helps us to give reverence, and awesomeness to God. The Holy Spirit is the one that convicts us and is to judge the world - John 16:8. Spiritual Living involves allowing God's fire of purification, and cleanliness from all unrighteousness. If we have the Holy Spirit in us, we can do greater and mighty things as he gives us power to do so ( Acts 2:3). The spirit of the Lord helps us to show mercy to others. His spirit gives us life , wisdom and understanding  and it quickens us the flesh does not profit us anything- John 6: 63. In the book of John, chapter14 verse 6 where Jesus said, "I am  the way, the truth and the life," It is the spirit of God in Christ that gives the life.

Disobedience to the word of God will cause so much harm to us just like a child who disobeys parents will not make their parents happy and always getting into trouble. Being

16

obedient to Gods work will only make us miss hell and make it to heaven. The importance of obedience cannot be overemphasized. In Genesis, if Adam and Eve obeyed God, there would not be suffering and dying but the moment they disobeyed him, everything changed for the worse. It is not the intention of God to make us suffer; it is the devil who deceives man to disobey God. Because of disobedience, we have all sorts of problems. We are faced with sickness and disease and tragedy in our lives since Adam and Eve disobeyed God. That's when our challenges started. It is only God who will take it away.

By living a spirit filled life, one can gain access to his presence and in his presence is full of joy, healing, salvation, freedom from sin, liberty and peace of mind and these things can be done in moderation. Let not your heart be troubled. Believe in God and also in me. When you feed your spirit being through prayers, fasting, meditating on his words, you will be able to stay strong. Our spiritual minds need spiritual food just as we all need physical food to survive. The bible says that those who live in the flesh cannot please the Lord.

What does it mean to live in the flesh?

Living in the flesh involves giving the flesh whatever it demands or desires, and fulfilling all sinful desires whether it is against the  will of God or not. Just go ahead and please the flesh. Doing what the flesh wants, eating what we want not even paying attention to any warning signs will lead to doom. Smoking is an example. There is a warning on the package but people still go on to smoke, not paying attention to the warning. I came across a young person, and we had a

17

discussion about healthy topics. The other person likes smoking a lot, and would not like to quit. He can quit other things but not smoking. He said, "I have no intention to quit smoking." Sometimes, we make decisions that affects us in one way or another, but its not too late to do things right. We should be controlled by the Holy Spirit rather than alcohol and drugs because the Holy Spirit makes us pure within and comes outside our lives. Certain things we consume in forms of food can hurt us. Now people, know the dangers associated with alcohol, and drug addiction. In order to be spiritually fit one should not let the Devil deceive us to make us eat or drink something that will cause physical or mental detriments. To be spiritually filled is to have the fruits of the Holy Spirit of which patience, self control, doing things in moderation and with the fear of God or long suffering is one of them. The Holy Spirit will control your appetite on what you eat or drink. This is why we need Him in our lives. In today's world, that is the last thing that occupies our minds. We are busy driving to games, football, work and so forth, but not in a hurry to get to church. There are increased road rages from drivers. No one wants the other to overtake them. Satan uses anything to build up his strong holds around our dwelling places, homes, offices and our communities. For instance, the issue of divorce is on the rise. No one wants to be patient and give each other time to change or do better. People get married and in one year or less there is divorce. One year is not enough for two different people to know everything about each other. You are just starting to live together. It does not matter how long you dated. Once people get married situations can change. But don't let it change your marriage and faith to one another. Allowing God first is very important in our daily lives and relation to one another. Husbands and wives should tolerate one another, give time to grow in the marriage and have a tool called, "patience." The devil uses this lack of patience to attack so many families today. Learning to be tolerant of each other especially in our relationship with one another even in our family or homes will go a long way to help our spiritual living and mindset. We should allow the word of God to take part in our lives and control our journeys by meditating on his word day and night. Most of us have time to do our hair, nail and to look beautiful on the outside. It is good to look pretty but we have to be pretty inside and outside especially our heart this is the seat of most of our actions. Taking care of our physical, mental and emotional health are all part of life, and its good. All of this is good but we need to make time to study the words of our Lord and Savior because His word is life and provides light onto our feet. The bible tells us that in John 3:16, "For God so loved the world that he gave his only begotten son that whosoever believe in him should not perish but have everlasting life." A simple act of obedience and acceptance of Christ in our lives is all we need to be acceptable to God. When our first parents sinned, they were chased out of the Garden of Eden and God being kind enough, decided to give us a second chance by sending Jesus Christ to come in the form of a baby born in a manger. He died in order to save us from our sins and bring us back to God again where everlasting life is guaranteed. Sometimes, it is not easy to do the right thing but with faith in him, we can do all things and with our Heavenly Father's support. Every one of us has a God given potential. All we need to do is to ask God to reveal it to us and make it manifest so that we can expand and produce fruits such as joy, peace, mercy and kindness to each other despite the color of our skin, the language spoken the height and academic qualifications and ability. We have to live like our father who is willing to forgive when we realize our sins, and confess to him. He promised to wash our sins even though they be as crimson, they will be as white as snow. We need to practice forgiveness, and humility in order to be filled. This is the question we can ask ourselves, "How often do we forgive one another?" It includes in the family or on the job. The bible says seventy times seven this means just forgive at all times, and let things go.

# *Chapter Two*

# *Humble Yourself*

OBEDIENCE- The act of being humble and loyal to authority doing what we are told to do. I used to work as a Charge Nurse of a hospital, and I remember making assignments and assigning job duties to other nurses. I was there to help, and make the job smooth and easy for other people. Now, if a nurse was disobedient, there were consequences that followed such as being written up or getting fired at worst cases. Of course, no one likes to be written up because it goes on the annual evaluation and would prevent some pay raises and so fort. Obedience is important, and it is practicing godliness in our everyday living just as cleanliness is next to Godliness. When we obey and trust God we are elevating him and he is happy with us but when we disobey and doubt his words we are belittling him. We have to elevate our Heavenly Father by putting our trust in Him. Life challenges comes, and he promises us a way of escape and victory that only comes from faith. Obeying the word of God and keeping his commandments by teaching our children and family the way of the Lord is very beneficial whether it is now or in the time to come.

**WALKING WITH GOD**

## Way to Go – Spiritual Living

It's amazing how a baby grows in the womb and when they are born, they go through the stages of development. It starts with growing from childhood to adulthood, and all the time the parents have to have patience. They are hopeful that their son or daughter will become a doctor or lawyer one day. Our Heavenly Father is also patient with us by giving us time to repent, and to grow. He wants us to grow, and develop physical and spiritually. The only thing required of us is to accept the gift of salvation which God gave us through His son, Jesus Christ. Working with God starts right where you are. It involves from the time you wake up till you go back to bed meditation of His words, praying every day, studying His words, saying your morning prayers with your family and involving the children. You can let them know about the Lord so that when they grow up, they will not forsake Him by asking the Holy Spirit to take control of the day for you. It is the Lord that keeps us as a city or as a nation. It is not by power nor might neither is it by educational level, how rich and poor we may be it is by His grace. Most of us grew up being raised by either our biological parents or otherwise in either way we learn by taking all advice our parents gave us. We were able to stand on our own as time went on from child to adulthood. When we were children, we behaved like children but now that we are adults we are expected to behave like adults, having responsibilities of father and mother to our children. You do not run away from your parental obligations. Raising kids is a blessing that we ought to be proud of and we should do it to the best of our ability. God gave us responsibility to train and raise those kids by living, and showing examples to the children.

The advice from parents is very important that is why the Bible tells us, "Obey your father and mother so that your days may be long." On the other hand, parents are advised not to provoke their children. We should love, and provide for our children at all times. The word of God has provision on how to live with one another. Parental obligations and everyone else responsibilities to accomplish. Children, do not neglect the advice from your parents because it is life for you. It is the way to go. We cannot see the principalities and powers but their action is controlling the world today and the action is spread across the globe. It is by our fervent prayer unto God that situations will change and chains can be broken, yolk of sickness, addiction, yolk of poverty and diseases.

## HOW CAN MEN AND WOMEN WALK WITH GOD?

Women and men have a lot of responsibilities at home especially our women. They need to be appreciated for their hard work providing for their families. In some cases, women are the bread winners when the husbands cannot and they are there for the children and the family, being supportive of their husbands, encouraging one another when there is no job, no money or no food. I was in a Bible class one time when a lady gave a testimony of how God provided for them. It was a family of three kids and the parents. The only food that the man could afford was squash and mushrooms because there was no job at that time. Even though there were not enough

23

to eat, the family had faith, patience and hope that one day things would be alright. The ability that God gave to our parents and the wisdom given to help in raising our children was phenomenal. It's hard work to raise kids. It's a known fact, "It takes a village to raise up children." It is not something you leave for one person to accomplish. Couples have to be there for each other by providing financial support, emotional help, communication, advice, protection of each other and all. In some families, the women did it by themselves with no spouse and the same goes for the men. Our mothers need to be commended and appreciated for their hard work by being there for the children at all times, being supportive providing food when the fathers are unable, taking care of the homes, juggling homework and job work. One thing that we don't know is that God will bless us for taking care of any child in your family or others who may need help. As women, when we perform our duties at home and we are encouraged to do it with joy and hope. Here in America, the parents have to help to make sure their kids complete their homework and this happening in all parts of the world. Homework has become a global thing even the pre-k kids all have homework and to make matters worse, some of our parents are single mothers and fathers so what do you do? You pray and ask for guidance and the grace to be able to be a prudent wife or husband to our kids and to protect our children from any harm from our environment. As parents, God has given us the ability to raise those kids in a God fearing environment by teaching them the word right from birth until they grow old themselves. I know our mothers have so much responsibility at home. They have to cook, clean, shop, provide delicious meals and other family assignments in order to maintain order and peace. The mothers also have to say prayers together as prayers will keep family together. It is good to have money to pay your bills but if we have money but no peace in the home the money itself may not help anyone we need the money and the peace that only Jesus can give to anyone that asks. And if we do not ask we are not going to receive. We need to learn to start asking God for anything in our prayers. Women have a part to play in making the home peaceful for habitation. Women are encouraged to bring peace into the homes even when the husbands cannot. We ought to represent our Heavenly Father by teaching our children the morals and showing them by examples, the way we live our lives and our values by maintaining self-worth and integrity, putting God first. All other things comes second. Instilling the value of respect in our culture, teaching the fear of God in our family and the way we do things, represent our Heavenly Father. By living a life of example, the way we dress and conduct ourselves whether in private or public to be good ambassadors of God and all. By living a life of prayer, respecting each other in the home and at our offices by working well with our coworkers can help. It is very important to incorporate the word of God in everything that we do in our daily lives even in our marriage and relationships with one another. This is important because the Bible says, "Your word is a lamp unto my path." It is by his word that we live and have our beings. We see by his word when we study the word, we are encouraged and persuaded to do his will. The word by the spirit of God shows us how to live holy and be the real godly sons and daughters of God. His word is sharper than a two-edged sword to break every yolk of alcoholism and immoralities. When we believe, we are given power to become the sons and daughters of God. We need power and grace to live as children of God. We need daily prayer power, daily living power to break the yolk of sin in our lives. The word has power to not only break the yolk of sin but demonic powers of operation, sickness and poverty. The word of God provides daily wisdom to guide you from day to day even how to conduct ourselves, how to say things to one another without causing anger and rage in others. The word comes with power, wisdom and understanding.

# *Chapter Three*

# *Daily Devotion Matter's*

We need spiritual food just as we feed ourselves with our regular food. The word of God is the food to the soul just as salads, and burgers feed our physical bodies. It is the word of God that will cleanse us from all unrighteousness. Daily prayers is an important thing we do as Christians just as Daniel in the Bible prayed three times a day. We should likewise do the same, and not be weary. We are urged to "Pray without ceasing." Let us not be weary in our daily prayers as the Lord instructed us because our adversary. The devil is so sneaky and has strong holds everywhere even in your family including your job, and other places you can think of. It is with the prayers that you can break all the yolk of poverty, sickness, disease and infirmity. A prayerless Christian they say is powerless. The word of God is life, and light to our feet. It is by this that we move and live by.

OBEDIENCE-The importance of obedience cannot be overemphasized we reap a lot of good results when we obey and humble ourselves. It is important to plant the seeds of obedience into our lives and family especially in our children. It is not only hearing the word of God, but being doers as well will give us eternal benefits which money cannot buy. Letting His word change our attitude, and behavior is number one. In the book of Isaiah, many blessing are promised to us as we remain obedient. "You shall eat the good of the land."


## ACCEPTANCE

ACCEPTANCE-Salvation is a free gift God gave to man by sending his only begotten son to die and save the world. We don't know how much it cost Him to see our sins nailed to that cross, and we cannot even afford it and to pay Him back. God wants all of us to repent from all our sins, and follow Him by accepting Him into our lives by giving the Holy Spirit the chance to dwell inside of us and minister to us at all times. Just as all of us are born in iniquity, it is important to be born again not by the will of the flesh but by the Holy Spirit. In order for us to see the Kingdom of God, we have to be born again by repentance from our sinful nature, asking for forgiveness and allowing Christ to dwell in us directing our affairs daily on this earth and make Jesus the savior of our lives. When we let Him be the controller of our lives, all of these problems will be handled by Him. There will be no discord in the family. Husbands will love their wives, and be the head of the family as God made it in the beginning. They should be there to protect, and nurture the family with the help of their wives. The issue of cheating, and divorce will not even be there if we give God a chance to rule. Any marriage that allows God to be in it will succeed because it's not by power or might neither is it by how much you have it is by the spirit of the Lord, the Bible says. We cannot do anything by our own power and wisdom. All things are made by him. It is God that gives wisdom to them that asks just as Solomon did in the Bible. He asked for wisdom and God gave him not only wisdom but also riches and glory. If anyone needs wisdom we should ask from the Lord as he is the owner of wisdom and we need Godly wisdom to live on this earth where God places us to inhabit. We need wisdom to live with one another even in our neighborhoods, communities, and families. Husbands should apply wisdom to deal with their wives. Children and teenagers need wisdom to go through life challenges. Going through puberty, and life changing through adulthood is not easy to handle therefore our youth needs wisdom. They will be able to deal with situations at school, peer pressure and in our home. They need our parental advice to succeed. Allowing God to direct our lives is very important decision to make. One question was asked by someone in a Sunday school class one time. The questions was, "What if I was raised by a pastor of a church, can that bring salvation to my soul?" The answer was, "Being raised by a pastor of a church will not bring salvation to our soul." Salvation is not passed from father to son it is obtained by acceptance of the Jesus Christ as Lord, and personal Savior and it is on individual basis. I was raised by a Christian parent but all these years I came to the realization that salvation is on individual basis. I have to work for my own salvation. The mother or father cannot work out salvation for their children, but we can lead them to Christ. A pastor of a church cannot transfer salvation to his or her children or church members. One has to single handedly confess with their mouth, and accept the Lord as our Lord and personal Savior.

## Way to Go – Spiritual Living

Has anyone wondered what it will be like to have everlasting life which only God can give or having everlasting joy that never ends? Walking with Him and doing the will of our father is the way to enter into his kingdom. We are so precious in his sight as John 3:16 says, "For God so loved the world that He gave his only begotten son that whosoever believes in Him should not perish but have everlasting life." It continues somewhere to say that the life is in his son. We are the only creatures that God made in his image. The other things, He spoke into existence we are actually the creation he took time to make and He gave us dominion over the earth to inhabit the whole earth. We need to obey the Lord in all we do with our body and soul. I was telling someone during one prayer session that if God chose to make us as stones, and rocks that is what we will be. We cannot change ourselves or our outward appearance. I know some people have the finance to go for plastic surgery for facial touch up and body reconstruction but some of those surgeries are expensive and more so have complications. No one can remake us. As the potter has the power over the clay which can be molded into different shapes and sizes and even all kinds of colors, he made us. The potter can change the style of the pot because he has the power. The clay doesn't have the power over the potter. We don't have power except the one God gave us. We don't have a spare life but God does and has promised to give us eternal life when we accept the Lord Jesus Christ as our savior by confessing our sins and forsaking them. By going to him, he promised to accept us as we are. Because we are his sheep, he will not cast us away. The Lord is calling all of us everywhere even in all languages, people of all sizes and shapes. It doesn't matter what religion you identify with, we are all his children. He is asking us to accept his gift of salvation to have a new life. The Lord is pleading for us to repent, confess your sins with your mouth and believe in your heart that Jesus is the son of God and thou shall be saved. It is as simple as that. It is not a hard thing to do. It is only the devil that wants us to think it is hard thing to do. Just a simple act of obedience by asking God to forgive our sins and asking Jesus to come into our lives and make the difference so that we can start walking with our Heavenly Father. We can do his will as he is not willing for any of us to perish but to have eternal life. Some of us make a list of what we accomplish in one day. For instance some people wake up as early as 5:00 am to get ready for work, school and other errands. I had a patient while I was working in a clinic he told us how he will get up very early to start getting ready for his appointment on time .Some people can get that early to the hospital but some will drag their feet to go to the house of God. In the bible David recalled he was " glad when they say let us go to the house of God" Going to the gym to work out and loose weight, shopping, getting our hair and nail dazzled, and watching television are all good things to do but the question is what time do we devote to studying God,s word, praying for our family and loved ones even our enemies as he wants us to do? If we don't study his words we cannot defeat the devil when he comes because Satan will quote the bible for someone remember when Jesus was on the earth after forty days of fasting the devil tempted him quoting some bible verses but because Jesus is the word he defeated him. We need the word of God daily in our lives just as people drink coffee in the morning the same way we need his word every day of our lives. We will defeat the devil by the word of our testimony.

This book was written to encourage us to start today it's never too late to start reading, studying and meditating on his words. We need to make time to study the word of God. When we study his word, he speaks to us and we learn a lot on how to live with each other. The bible has enough words for all of us. It has sections for men, women even children and teenagers. It will do us good to read this Bible because other worldly books cannot bring us closer to God but the Bible will. That is how important it is. In the world that we live in, we go through tons of challenges. Some of us were born from poverty and some made their riches by hard work and still most challenges can be overcome but they are not completely wiped away. The world is controlled by satanic forces which we cannot even see by the naked eye. It is only the spiritual eye that observes spiritual things this is why we need a spirit filled life, filled by the power of the Holy Spirit at all times. The solution to our marital problems are not cheating or getting new husbands and wives every time something happens, we need to learn to fix things in our home just like whenever something breaks in the house, a handyman comes to take a look at things to fix we need to be vigilant and observe things and learn to fix it before it goes really bad. It's like having a leak in the home and one ignores it. The leak may eventually cost you the house you suffered to get so being observant in the things going on around you and family is very helpful. We need to stand up and allow the spirit of the Lord to help us deal with all type of challenges.

The Lord is coming soon and we all know that God is not a person that he can lie. When he said it, he mean it. We got to be prepared for the Lord's coming. Jesus said he is going to prepare a place for us and after that, he will come and gather us for himself. We have to be serious with our belief in him and trust him to stand by his word. Just like a bridegroom wants his bride to be dressed in clean white garments, not filthy, but clean and ready during the day of the wedding. No man expects for his wife to be dirty or dressed up in pajamas on a wedding day. He wants us to be fully dressed in our white garment of righteousness waiting for him. We cannot be filthy for our father by the way we live, behave, actions and not being alert to his coming.

## USING THE SYSTEMS OF OUR BODY FOR GOD to honor him

We are made in the likeness of God. All his creations are good including man and woman and all the wisdom and knowledge we have is from God. We need to take care of the body he gave us from head to toe every part of our body should be for his worship. The thoughts that comes to our mind our father knows them and gave us a choice to choose good and bad. As children of God let us choose good and not bad thoughts because he knows our thoughts. When we think something in our hearts, God knows. Our mouth is important tool in our body we need to guard our mouth and refrain from speaking evil to one another but speak positive and blessings to people we meet. The things that we say with the mouth, we will give account to God. All the things that we ever said, we must be careful what comes out of it. It is important that we watch what we say to one another. For some people who like to gossip, please consider speaking positive things and not negative talk. Render a helping hand instead of gossiping about your co- worker or each other. Talk more about what you see with our eyes. God gave us eyes to see and he can see more than us. It is important to be careful what we look at too. For example, it will not give God praise when we continually watch pornography as this pollutes our minds with worldly desires. This will leave negative impacts on our children because these children will grow up doing the same thing that their parents did. I listened to one of the court cases on TV one day. The parents loved  watching pornography and they did not realize the kids are watching and learning their way. One day it happened that the computer was available for the kid to use and  this child started watching same thing as the parents. We have very big responsibilities in raising these children so we should not take it for granted. It is a very high position to be a parent raising one or more children. They were given to you to raise them up in the way of the Lord so that when they grow up, they will not forsake the Lord. We should guard our hearts because all evil thoughts come from the heart. We should be alert at all times to make sure that we are not thinking evil for no one because God can read our heart like letter. Coming to our hands in

## Way to Go – Spiritual Living

Genesis, God made the heavens and the earth and he rested on the seventh day. Now, if God worked it means we ought to do something with our hands to make a living. Men and women need to be able to provide for their families especially their children. Men should be bold and stand up to their fatherly responsibilities of raising the children providing food and shelter for them and loving the wife that God gave them. Everything is a gift from God and we should never take anything for granted. Wives are to be obedient to their husbands and be submissive as the Bible wants us to. Putting God first in the marriage and walking with the Lord in your marriage is the best thing any couple will do. The Lord does not want us to be lazy, he wants us to work and earn a living he promised to help us along the way of life. This book is encouraging all of us to utilize all our being in obedience to his words. Our feet should not be fast in running to do bad stuff or to partake some crimes. We should not partake in it. Our kids should not partake in it as well. All parts of our body from our head to toe has a purpose and functions to what God wants us to use it for the temporary time we have on the earth. Is like giving one million dollars to a person to start a business and after a while the business owner comes back and wants account and balancing. The Bible says we will give account of all that we did with our body even the things we said to other people and hurt their feelings. We need to ask God to give us the power to live a holy life and it is the spirit of the Lord that will enable us to live a holy life. His spirit guides us and helps us to do his will. Its not by our power or might. It is only by his spirit.

## PATIENCE

PATIENCE- This word is not in some people's vocabulary. Today, the world and the people are in so much hurry to get to their destination and speeding has killed so many people and caused a lot of havoc in our life. Many accidents occur due to speeding. As soon as one drives out of the driveway , there are cars racing from different directions and road rage is on the rise on our road, people overtaking each other. It does not matter how fast you go, some people will be faster than others. I just happened to be driving along the two way lane on the road one day and two cars passed by me one after another in few seconds. Did not realize the reason was they were trying to be on the lane closer to their exit. But I realized the importance of having this quality of a Christian life called patience. Learning to tolerate one another and exercising patience in our life matters a lot in our relationship and family. There was a saying that "a patient dog eats the fattest bone." God is patient with us he does not kill us the first time we sin, therefore we should incorporate this quality in our life and teach it to our children.

# *Chapter Four*

# *Planting Crop*

## FRUITS OF THE HOLY SPIRIT

FRUITS OF THE HOLY SPIRIT- When we plant crops it is expected to grow and germinate and produce seeds. We will not be happy to see our plant not germinating. Some of us can buy Miracle Grow for the plant to grow. Most people work hard to make their yard look the best in a neighborhood planting and putting fertilizer and doing so many things to make the yard look pretty. The miracle grow we need is the holy spirit . He is the one that will direct our ways and help us to grow in the Lord and cleanse us from all unrighteousness. Bearing the fruits of the Holy Spirit is important. As God's children living by example teaching and changing lives, and building up and uplifting each other as one builds a house. Many of us know that to build a house you need to start laying the foundation with bricks then continue until the house becomes what we want in size and shape. We are required to build up one another by showing love and kindness and not hate. We cannot build up by hate and negative talk to or about one another. When we show love to one another, we are known as the children of God and it is one of the fruits of the Holy Spirit. Love is the greatest of all and God is love. He who cannot love is not of God.

37

## Way to Go – Spiritual Living

What if we move mountains and do great things in life without loving one another? It will be in vain. We ought to show love and respect to one another starting from where you are in the family, office, shopping centers and other places even in our places of worship. It is love that brought Jesus to die on the cross in order to save the whole world. He is asking for us to accept him today and let him be the Lord of your life. Love and humility is very important in the life of any Christian.


OBEDIENCE- One of the works of the Holy Spirit is to encourage us to obey. The word says, "The spirit leads us to obey." The importance of obedience cannot be over emphasized. When we obey God, there are blessings attached to it. Disobedience on the other hand has its own consequences. The earth was cursed when Adam disobeyed God. No parent is happy when kids disobey them. Same goes with our heavenly father. We have to obey God and keep his commandments . Jesus said in the bible" If you love me keep my commandments. We cannot serve God and Satan at the same time, we have to make time for the things of God, such as bible reading, prayer, meditation. It is important to have the fear of God in our lives and always teach our children "One cannot serve two masters at a time." You either please one or displease another. We cannot serve Satan at the same time and serve God. We need to make up our minds to serve God and be called God's children. In some countries where they have kings and queens they have a special way how the citizens will bow and greet them. This is earthly kings. But how much more the king of Kings which is Jesus he deserves our worship and obedience to his word. The Lord is our provider and we need to respect him with all our substance. He wants us to be obedient to his words and be holy because he is holy. Applying modesty in the things we do is the perfect example. Being good stewards of the things given to us to keep.

## THE CONSEQUENCES OF SIN

Question: "What are the consequences of sin?"Answer: There are lots of consequences that follow sinful acts. For instance, when our first parents, Adam and Eve sinned, first of all, they were ashamed and eventually were driven out of the Garden. Sin brings shame on us. It takes us away from God, the Father and when we are away from God, "Guess who will be near us," Satan the devil! He is the killer and the accuser of the brethren. Jesus told us in the Bible, "I have come that you may have life and have it more abundantly." Satan came to destroy and kill us. It is not the will of God for us to die young, it is the will of Satan because he is a destroyer and killer. We should not give Satan the chance to come near our family, children or even our churches because when he comes in he will cause a lot of havoc. When we sin we are close to the devil and very far from God. When this happens Satan is empowered when we obey and listen to him . Sin separates us from God and the ultimate - and severest - consequence of sin is death. The Bible says that "The wages of sin is death but the gift of God is eternal life through Jesus Christ the Lord," according to Romans 6:23. This not only refers to physical death, but to eternal separation from God in hell. "But your iniquities have separated you from your God, your sins have hidden His face from you, so that He will not hear. It's the foremost consequence of man's rebellion against God. Yet many want to believe that God is so "loving" that He will overlook our "little sins," such as lying and cheating and deceits even stealing no matter how small little white lies, cheating on the tax return, taking that pen when no one is looking, or secretly viewing pornography - taking your neighbors things or in some villages removing the landmark these are called sin. "They're not worthy of death, right?" The problem is that sin is called sin whether big or small. Though God loves us, God is a holy one that he cannot co- mingle with sin. You cannot prepare a fresh soup and try to mix it up with a sour soup. I am sure no one will like the taste. And so it is with sin ,it cannot be mixed with righteousness. Sin is like giving a shower to a pig, those of us who worked on the farm knows how hard it is to keep pig from going back in the dirt. Try to clean the pig and it will return right back into the mud. The mud is like a sin. God in his holiness is such that he cannot live with evil. The book of prophet Habakkuk describes God this way "Your eyes are too pure to look on evil it continue to say you cannot tolerate wrong." Habakkuk 1:13, God does not ignore our sin on the contrary, "You may be sure that your sin will find you out." Numbers 32:23 even those secret sins we hide in the hidden places of our heart, will one day be exposed "Nothing in all creation is hidden from God's sight. Everything is uncovered and laid bare before the eyes of Him to whom we must give account." Hebrew4 verse13.Paul made it abundantly clear that sin has consequences: "Do not be deceived: God cannot be mocked. A man reaps what he sows." You cannot sow corn and expect to reap apples. Of course, it will not work like that. God has given us principles to abide by and he is offering a freewill gift through his son Jesus Christ. Acceptance is willingly, it is not by force but he wants all of us to be saved and make it to his kingdom because he first loved us despite our sinful nature. Gal 6:7, this is where Paul then describes the end of those who indulge in sinful behavior: "The one who sows to please his sinful nature, from that nature will reap destruction" Gal 6 verse 8.But if we sow to the spirit we will reap everlasting life. The sinful nature refers to unrepentant self. Though the sinful nature may promise fulfillment, it can result suppressing the truth the consequence of it is that God gives the sinner over to "the sinful desires of their hearts," "shameful lusts" and "a depraved mind" as seen in Romans 1:24. The other consequences of sin is that God may allow the sinner to serve as his own god and to reap the destruction of his body and soul and it is a dangerous and fearful thing to be "given over" to our own destructive ways that is doing whatever our flesh desires and not paying attention to what the bible says. The answer is to repent today when you read this book.

When Jesus first began  his earthly ministry his first words were, "The time has come. The kingdom of God is near. Repent and believe the good news Mark 1:15. What is the good news? "For God so loved the world that He gave His one and only Son, that whoever believes in Him shall not perish but have eternal life" John 3:16 and it continue to say that this life is in his son. The consequence of sin is death,

Way to Go – Spiritual Living

but "the gift of God is eternal life in Christ Jesus our Lord" Romans 6: 23. The bible says if we neglect such a wonderful gift of salvation, we have ourselves to blame. God has given all of us another chance. When the first opportunities was messed up by the act of sin, he devised another means of getting us closer to him again by bringing a messiah in the name of our Lord and Savior, Jesus Christ. He is only asking for us to confess our sins to God today and acknowledge that you are a sinner. Ask for Jesus to come into your life and make the difference. Turn away from all the evil thing or criminal activities and ask for forgiveness , turn and follow Jesus! Don't go back to continue with the sins. Believe in your heart that he is the savior and you will be saved. Anyone who reads this book, I pray that the Lord will touch your heart to repent and accept the Lord Jesus in your life today and make the decision today to accept him and you will have everlasting life. Let us incorporate the fear of God in our lives, in our homes, offices and in relating to one another. The Holy Spirit is the one who helps us to have the fear of God in our hearts and when we have fear in our hearts, we will not do the will of the devil. The devil does not want us to fear God. He brings all kinds of confusion and lies to our hearts. The Devil is a deceiver the Bible says. He is the one who told Eve to eat the fruit in the Garden of Eden and he also told them that their eyes will be opened. He contradicts what the Lord hates. Our father hates lies but Satan is the father of lies. We need to have the fear of God in our homes, marriages, our work places, in our nations because without the fear of God, we cannot please our Heavenly Father. Young people should learn to fear God

42

because the fear of God is the beginning of wisdom, Proverbs 1:7. It is the foundation of true knowledge, it is only fools that will despise instruction. The fear of God makes us great people or nation. God blesses any nation that fears him and protects them from war and calamities. In the book of Psalm 112:1 the man that fear the Lord is called blessed. We are encouraged to fear the Lord and keep his commandments. "If you love me, keep my commandment," Jesus said to his disciples. The fear of God will keep us from sinning against him. When we fear God, we will not cheat on people, or take advantage of other people. We will do things in moderation. We will help those who need help because whatever you do for someone who cannot afford it, you will do it for God and he will reward you. There are so many benefits or rewards from fearing the Lord such as long life, prosperity, salvation, protection from evil and greatness. We receive his forgiveness and mercy of God, he is our protector, provider and our great deliverer when we fear him. It is a good thing to fear the Lord. It is like telling a kid to do some house chores and if the child loves and obeys the parents he or she will do what the parents says do. The parents will be happy with the child for being obedient and respecting them. We ought to respect God. He is our maker and he brought salvation and eternal life to us. It is up to us to accept or reject the offer but he is asking for everyone to accept him today and have everlasting life. Fearing God brings his pity and mercy on us and when that happens, his anger is turned away. Fearing God brings long life to us. Proverb 10:27. It brings answers to our prayers. It makes us acceptable unto him. It brings us closer to him. In The book of Daniel 6:26, when the king saw that the God of Daniel delivered him from the fire, he declared that everyone should worship and fear the God of Daniel. God had so many blessings which we cannot comprehend, that he is asking for us to fear and respect him. If we have fear of God we will not commit any crimes against our neighbors or inside the church of God. As parents, there are needs to instill the fear of God in our children to live so that they will begin a good life. The fear of God is for our protection. Reverencing God brings blessings that we cannot mention here in this book. When we fear God, we hate sins because our Father is holy therefore his children must be holy. This book is encouraging everyone to have the fear of God starting right where you are in the home, family even your marriages including places like where we work and in any relationship you have with others. Husbands and wives should have the fear of God in their marriage. Students and teenagers need the fear of God in their lives to keep them safe and prevent them from getting involved in any acts of sin. It is the fear of God that helps us to overcome sin and temptations and we inherit his blessings if we fear him and keep his commandments.

## WHY WE SHOULD PRAY

WHY WE SHOULD PRAY – One of the fruits of the holy spirit is the power of prayer. In Thessalonian 5:17, it tells us to pray without ceasing. Someone may ask the question – "Why should we pray when God is in control of everything in our lives and he is the controller of the whole world?" These are some reasons why we should pray. It is like the air we breathe and without air we cannot survive so it is with our prayers. It is the spiritual air we breathe which circulates to our physical being. It is better to pray than not to pray. When we pray, we obey the Lord's commandment. It is a way of serving the Lord. In Luke 2:36-38, Jesus taught us how to pray. When we pray our Lord's prayer, it is worthwhile. We pray to be rooted in the lord and to remain spiritually strong. It is the spirit of the Lord that gives us power to pray. Many things happen when we pray. Principalities and power will bow down with our prayers. It is a tool for our Christian race. Our prayers are like the money you keep in the bank for later use, to pay bills and other things for the future. The prayers we offer today will break future yolks. If we don't pray nothing happens. In James 4:2, it says we don't receive because we did not pray.

Prayer is a way of digging into his presence. We are encouraged to pray for everything ourselves including family, children, friends, coworkers and for peace and joy for our nation and leaders. Our prayer helps us to establish a relationship with God. It helps us to determine God's will and direction for our lives. Jesus constantly went to God in prayer and Daniel prayed 3 times a day to God. When we pray and bring every issue to God, he will handle it for us. Mark 13:33 tells us to watch and pray for we do not know when the time will come for Jesus to return. It is not only asking God for one thing or another our prayer is a way of maintaining a closer relationship with our Heavenly Father. Just like when people are in marriage, there are things they do to keep the marriage going, so it is with prayers. It allows God to change our will to confirm to his own will. There are many reasons why we should pray:

# Way to Go – Spiritual Living

Personal reasons - We need to pray for our personal needs, good health, healing for our body, salvation, promotion on a job, peace and blessings, protection from all evil, wisdom and grace from God to live with one another.

Family- Our family needs our prayers for protection, from the plans of the enemy, and the environmental factors. Our children need our prayers most for God's protection in their lives. Our nation needs prayers to seek the face of God to help choose the best leader for the nation. We must pray for everything. Nothing is too big or too small to pray for and we should teach our children and family members how to pray because prayer opens doors that no man can open or close. It changes things and situations. It is a way of fellowshipping with God in our prayers. By prayer we receive strength, comfort, and other life resources both naturally and spiritually. Just as we breathe our air to live, we need prayer to sustain us spiritually. Prayer helps us resist temptations. Matthew 26:41, Jesus warned his disciples to "always watch and pray so you don't fall into temptations". Prayer is very important to our lives now both young and old people are encouraged to pray so they don't fall into those traps. When we pray, we bring God's presence on the Earth to do things and change situations as well as reveal God's mind which keeps us closer to him. Our nation needs our prayers to wedge wars, to maintain peace and to stop environmental hazards. We are required to pray for our leaders so they can lead us in a godly way because in the book of Zachariah, with God all things are possible not by might nor power but it is by the spirit of the Lord through our prayers. The mountains of problems in our lives would be leveled by our prayers so that situations can change. Prayer brings about salvation to our souls. It changes our financial situations, joblessness, homelessness, cancer, hiv or any other sickness that can be treated through prayers. Prayer is a weapon and a tool in the hand of a Christian to wedge war against principalities and powers. We need to be spiritually alert and vigilant because our enemy is very sneaky! We don't know when he will strike but our prayers will destroy him. God wants us to ask but if you don't ask you will not receive anything. God will miraculously change things and situations through our prayers. We will be amazed of what God will do and how things will change for the better.


## SUMMARY

This book is written to encourage everyone to accept the Lord Jesus into their lives. God loves us so much that he doesn't want us to perish, and he gave his only begotten son to come to the world and die. He rose up and went back to heaven to prepare a place for us and he will return back to this earth to take us with him. There is need for everyone to receive this gift! If we reject the son of God, we will be given the eternal punishment but if we confess our sins today and accept the Lord Jesus in our lives and let him be the Lord of our paths, we will be saved. The word of God is true and God cannot lie because he is not human. It does not matter what religion you are into right now but God is asking for everyone to accept Jesus in their life. Today, as you read this book, confess your sins to God, ask for forgiveness and then ask for the Lord to come into your life and change whatever

## Way to Go – Spiritual Living

you need. Continue to live for Christ. Jesus will come back to this earth. He said it and he will accomplish it. We need to be prepared for his return. We will not be filthy for him to accept us. We have to be washed by the blood of the Lamb by repenting and turning away from our sins and living for him in our daily lives. Just as it was in the days of Noah, people did not believe that it would happen and God is giving us a long time to repent. Some people said, " They have been saying this for a long time." We believe by faith that God will do whatever he said he would do. Jesus is coming back again! Please repent and  accept him today and  let him be the Lord of your life You will be happy with the decision! Please say this prayer of repentance: "Dear Lord, I admit I am a sinner and Jesus came and died on the cross for me. I am sorry for my sins and please forgive me, cleanse me from all unrighteousness and filthiness. Come into my life today as I accept you into my life. Takeover the leadership of my life from this day forward and for the rest of my life – Amen."

## *About the Author*

The author of this book was born and raised in Nigeria. By God's grace, I moved to America to join my wonderful husband, Chris. We are blessed with four children. I was born to late, Pastor Joseph Nwoke of Umuakam Afugiri Umuahia Abia State Nigeria. My Dad was an ordained pastor of The Apostolic Church. He was a preacher and loved the Lord. God used him to perform miracles. A lot of people, and churches were converted to God because of his work.

Way to Go – Spiritual Living
## *Fountain of Life Publishers House*

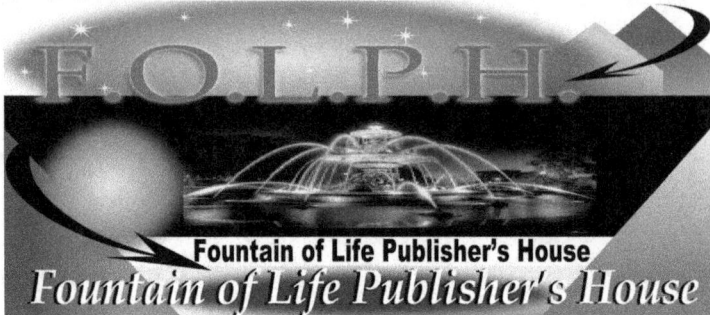

**Fountain of Life Publisher's House**

**P. O. Box 922612, Norcross, GA 30010**
**Phone: 404.936.3989**

**For book orders or wholesale distribution**

**Website:** www.pariceparker.biz

# Way to Go – Spiritual Living

www.ingramcontent.com/pod-product-compliance
Lightning Source LLC
LaVergne TN
LVHW051712080426
835511LV00017B/2875